Beagles

by Grace Hansen

abdopublishing.com

Published by Abdo Kids, a division of ABDO, P.O. Box 398166, Minneapolis, Minnesota 55439.

Printed in the United States of America, North Mankato, Minnesota.

052016

092016

Photo Credits: iStock, Shutterstock, Thinkstock

Production Contributors: Teddy Borth, Jennie Forsberg, Grace Hansen

Design Contributors: Dorothy Toth, Laura Mitchell

Cataloging-in-Publication Data

Names: Hansen, Grace, author.

Title: Beagles / by Grace Hansen.

Description: Minneapolis, MN : Abdo Kids, [2017] | Series: Dogs. Set 2 | Includes bibliographical references and index.

Identifiers: LCCN 2015959122 | ISBN 9781680805147 (lib. bdg.) | ISBN 9781680805703 (ebook) | ISBN 9781680806267 (Read-to-me ebook)

Subjects: LCSH: Beagle (Dog breed)--Juvenile literature.

Classification: DDC 636.753--dc23

LC record available at http://lccn.loc.gov/2015959122

Table of Contents

Beagles

Beagles are quick and **curious**. They have an excellent sense of smell. Beagles follow their noses wherever they go!

Beagles are small but **sturdy** hound dogs. They are about 1 foot (30.5 cm) tall at the shoulders. They have long, pointed tails.

Beagles have round, brown or **hazel** eyes. They have floppy ears. Their noses are black.

Beagles can be any hound color. But the tricolor beagle is the most common. Tricolor beagles are white, tan, and black.

A beagle's smooth, **dense** coat is rain **resistant**. Its coat is thicker in winter. This makes for lots of fur!

Grooming & Exercise

Beagles shed, but not too much. Brushing them weekly will help. Cleaning their ears regularly is important, too.

Beagles need their exercise. They love to go on daily brisk walks. Beagles must be leashed. If they pick up a scent, they will follow it!

Food & Play

Beagles love to eat. Their noses lead them to tasty treats. Food and garbage should be kept out of reach.

Beagles do not like to be alone for too long. They are friendly, fun, and love to play. So lots of time with their families is important!

More Facts

- Beagles do not make the usual barking sound. It is more like a quick, short howl.
- Beagles were first bred to track rabbits and hares. They are still used for this today.
- Beagles are often used for security purposes. Their sense of smell is amazing. But they are also very cute and friendly! So people feel comfortable around them.

Glossary

curious – eager to learn or know.

dense – having parts that are close together.

hazel – a color that combines brown, green, and gray.

resistant – capable of withstanding the effect of something.

sturdy – strongly built.

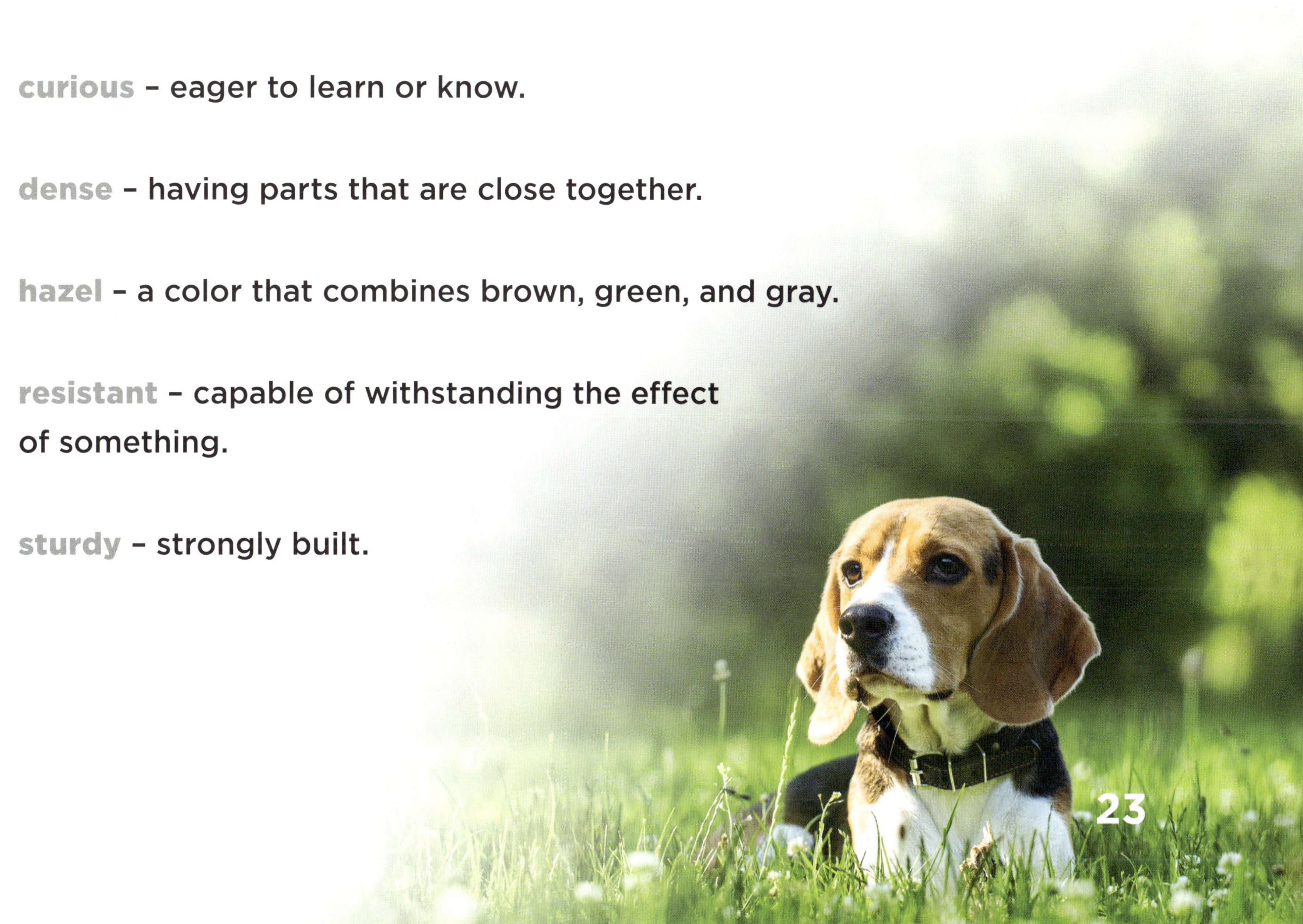

Index

abdokids.com

Use this code to log on to abdokids.com and access crafts, games, videos and more!